The Observances

Kate Miller grew up in Hampshire and now lives in London. She studied Art History at King's College, Cambridge, and Fine Art at Central St Martin's College of Art and Design, London. In 2012 she completed a PhD at Goldsmiths, University of London, where she taught in the English department. She has received a number of awards including the Edwin Morgan International Poetry Prize in 2008. Selected for the 2011 and 2013 Salt *Best British Poetry* anthologies, her poems have appeared in journals including *Poetry Review*, *The Rialto*, *The SHOp*, *Warwick Review* and the *TLS*, to which she also contributes an occasional introduction to a 'Poem of the Week'. This is her first volume of poetry.

KATE MILLER

The Observances

OxfordPoets

CARCANET

First published in Great Britain in 2015 by
Carcanet Press Limited
Alliance House
Cross Street
Manchester M2 7AQ

www.carcanet.co.uk

We welcome your comments on our publications
Write to us at info@carcanet.co.uk

A CIP catalogue record for this book is available from the British Library

ISBN 978 1 90618 815 3

The publisher acknowledges financial assistance from Arts Council England

Typeset by XL Publishing Services, Exmouth
Printed and bound in England by SRP Ltd, Exeter

for my father

Here on this ring of grass we have sat together...
The trees wave, the clouds pass. The time approaches
when these soliloquies shall be shared.

Virginia Woolf

Contents

1 WAVE ... CLOUDS PASS

2 LIFE CLASS

3 VIGILS

4 ENTER THE SEA

WAVE ... CLOUDS PASS

1

Regarding a Cloud

In the ground is an eye,
satined and turtled,
regarding a cloud.

It studies the scene
from a patch in the earth
and reflects: I am part of that sky.

Just a picnicker's spoon
with no handle, exposed
by a scalping of growth,

and it's upside down,
mortared in mud – as jewels
were set in the eyeholes of gods

till they fell from the temples.
No-one thought twice about
gouging them free.

But it must be earthed here,
as Antony says, to 'amplify
concentration'

holding the trees in its stare,
balancing us on its shell.

Promise

The earth is scanty over London
clay, sour with runoff, a swollen underpass
of beige.
        I hoped it would be sweet enough
for planting but already I'm forgetting
the purpose of my dig.

        As a child I'd fossick
at the beach or down the garden,
reluctant – family photos show – to pose,
back turned against the camera, absorbed,
uncovering what lay below
                        not far below.

        Now pebbles come to light,
they bob up like small heads.
I shuck them free of soil, saved
from the stew of bones, sewer pipe,
hardcore, next door's
                   tossed–over glass.

        With thumb and fingertips
I clean a clutch of gluey eggs
– such promise
              in their ovoid forms, damp
shells – although the shine's ephemeral:
they never feel like stones.

        As shingle used to
yield its netsukes,
            and sand its curios,
so even this poor ground is inexhaustible.

The Long Goodbye

You always had a way with clouds,
as if they'd started life with you, coddled
in your arms, reared out of bonfire
smoke or hay-steam from baked fields.

Landscape painters looked to you to catch
the best effects, clouds like leopards,
lions, the great processions of a Byzantine
October. Now there's little call for craft.

Or colour – years since you bore flowers
and drifted suns of pollen on the earth.
Tip up your grizzled chins and sky-watch.
Suck on your many pipes and offer me

bassoon pronouncements
on the drought, a fray of cirrus,
freakishness of hail, last hurricane.
Your old scars map a century of weather,

the haul of water, how you leaned
aslant the wind. You stand a long time
dying, but before you die, old tree,
let's drink another rain.

Lines To Convey Distance

Send me one hundred greys to catch
the chill and whip of water,
all those marine and aerial greys
for squalls, cloud, waves
in every cast of light,

also to catch the skirling
marks of different flights
when birds take off in pairs or flocks,
their streamlines paying out,

and put in samples of some even finer
greys, close quiet tones to suit
hunched blots of waders
who inspect their yards of mud
for life, singletons, rain–dark.

Longest Day

Before you leave, before the sea returns,
we draw out our walk as far
from houses and the spire as we dare,
collecting samphire,
salt jade for the passage out.

It grows on mud between the hulls
where broken boats have gone to grass,
become the settled parishes of wood and weeds
I hoped would anchor us.

And still we speak of journeying and home
in port and starboard words
until the pilot buoys and off-shore lights
begin to roll the estuary tar-sleek,
a metalled road beneath first stars.

Nightfall on the longest day
– it doesn't fall. Detaches,
lifts the warmth away.

Every Book is a Long Walk

I remember starting one, a worn green hardback
on a headland, warmed by sun but little visited.

If at first I skipped a page, my eye was met
by black-lashed wild pansies,
staring from the carpet in the dunes.

Here were horses, scrapping gulls – much like the book.
Two characters slipped off along a Baltic beach,
I sat by the Atlantic.

Scanning the sea he talked of prospects,
life not bound by trappings,
pastimes or the filial duties of their age.

And she believed the freedom he proposed
would suit her, à la mode and bridal
in the streaming lace of waves.

I closed the book. I walked and saw her faintly,
filmy in the shallows – then braving coarser surf,
undone to her shift and shivering,

grey as in a mirror
in an unfrequented room – passing
to and fro, passed by

as if she were the shoreline
ceding to, emerging from the tide.

Couple in the Park with No Kids

Beyond the scratchy skirt of yews
my ambling dog has nosed, a couple lies
engrossed, half-screened (have they skipped work?)

pleasure-seeking in the dusty earth.
High-shine, two cans askew in grass have given them away.

Flies graze,
a self-effacing moth lifts itself
off scabious, those pale, heavy-headed flowers.

At Kew one August we lay likewise side by side
on tombs, behind a pall of rhododendrons. That afternoon

a pride of pregnant women bloomed
along the gravel paths, juggernauts of happy families
drove swags of babies past.

No Place

Did you kip here on this lakeside bench, hunched
kid with pepper hair? You're shaking, are you scared?
Those are holes in your black trainers? Just begun
your London life by sleeping rough? (I'm trying not to stare.)
You're deaf to my 'Hello' and dumb.
Eyes down, we both look sorry, blind to the pair
of crested grebes, crooked like question-marks, who skim
to a deserted clump of reeds, their nest year after year.

The Hoopoes Have Come Home

My father calls. He interrupts me
folding down a family of shirts and stiffened sheets.
He says the hoopoes have come
home. His eye is on them

now: they strut between the pines, prospecting,
always doubling back to that
patch where the tower burned.
With banded heads like hammers

they fine-pick in the dirt – wrecking
where we used to sit; in spring, he sighs,
it's only briefly green until the hoopoes come.
Time for his old lament (I fumble

the refrains) about the birds, forgiven
for their grubbing-up but never
letting him forget this was *their* field,
ditch and scrub he cleared for house, sheds, folly.

City birds, I say, behave as if our backyards
were the hood: crow speared another frog,
jays squabble three doors down, starlings
scrape gutters for the moss,

and all the while I'm watching skipping tits forsake
the ivy's closeness and flit
quick, flicker like matches lighting.
I do not ask after Mother.

Against This Light

You ask me, Marie-Amélie, am I the youth
who said goodbye last month?
                                                    To answer you
I'll paint myself against this light, immersed in
your first words from home, tempered in the blaze of blue
and gold that is an April sky in Rome.
In my high-ceilinged room the window opens
on a crinkled map of roofs and parapets.
Swallows clip the sill. In their bright air
I thrive.
                    I ache to think of you – confined,
the Cast Room stove not lit since Easter,
among the plaster limbs the master favours – frozen
forms I've left behind.
                                        Everything I see
if I go down to watch the market in the Campo
moves: knives and scales flash at fish stalls
decked with lemons, to the thrum of forge and stable,
fresh stone-dust loads loaves and cheeses, and a girl
in carmine slips into the shade beyond a column,
out of the flap of sun-bleached linen.
                                                            I own I've fallen
more than half in love with Romans. Young or old,
they hold themselves as proud as any figure in a frieze.
I'm hungry for the way a woman turns her head,
the telling language of a trader's hand.
Alive or carved, they're definite and grand,
even in the shadows of an alley, warm.

all'antica

Hot with pink, fruit trees strip, slop blossom
on the rubble wall, when out [through garage doors]

across our path is thrust the gleaming barrel
of a mare – not a battered *motorino* – oiled

flanks, arched tail swinging from the bronze
rump like a sign above a shop.

Her handler's swearing as she bucks,
hooves ringing on the stones.

Between the trees stooped gardeners turn to look,
then go on, unconcerned, the tools to hand

unaltered since the year the Empress indulged
her husband's whim for orchards.

On Lower Marsh, the Wallflowers

self-seeded, streaky oxblood/English
mustard, breeze along hot bricks
in sunshine. Their sweet smell of sherbet
coaxes from the pissed-on wall
another possibility:
                              substitute hibiscus
for the small pink swimsuit
draped where it was found and left
to fade.
                  Under the arches in olive green
a man shouts out he always likes to
see a woman's collarbones. Only
April but she's taking off her cardigan
to be presented with a sheaf,
liver-dark in her white arms,
of wallflowers.

Not Dormant Now, *la Belle au bois*

If you want her, try the attic
where she won't be dressed much longer
in a painting shirt, old canvas shoes.

She's all for mingling
in the evening's *passeggiata*
among a crowd in pink and gold

escorted by a crocodile of cupids
on little clouds that sail
from Titian to the Biennale.

She's going to ride in water taxis
to and from Murano,
squander all her savings

on a longed-for chandelier.
I guess when she returns
she'll keep the house and garden

just as crummy as the locals do
in Venice. Let the cupboards smell
of must! I don't believe she ever will

replace that red ill-tempered rose
with one less spiky. Anyway, she rather likes
the scratch of briars on glass.

Passage

Within the wood a century is all
      but lost, graves overgrown, headstones
   tumbled, going-nowhere stairs,
   disconnected from the distant dome and towers,
      the rush of comfort from a passing train.

Wind and a pigeon hurry overhead
      along green pipes of ash and elder.
   Two branches hold the moment of their passage,
         lacing, give them lease, like lungs.
   Two paths diverge.

One leads a slow life
      lying lush beneath the polished ivy,
   the other has a pelt of sorts,
   a rug of mulch, rag and bone of littered leaf.
      Dog detects a trot of fox, the stop of feet.

And the path you'll take
      meanders. Punts its snaky trace through weed,
   as a boat – responding to the river's pull –
cleaves a road, rich and dark as bread, that carries someone home
      at first light, before green closes over.

2

LIFE CLASS

Patient at Paimio

Dusk lasts till midnight, dawn lights up at two,
long-drawn days – I follow Keats
and *if a sparrow come before my window*
I take part in its existence
and pick about... On this path lingonberries
grow, where needles drop from feathered pines
to lie in rafts, browning, as my fellows do,
on the sun decks of our forest ship.

We never seek landfall – only I
take in the creak of woodland, thump of water
in the purifying plant, bird squawk, infrequent
engine thrums. A laugh drifts from the sauna
– some acrid edge of resin in the steam
triggers the old impulse to cough
as if bacilli kept on doubling daily,
shoving, crowding into the lift of my lung.

After the sweats, white nights, snow-blank
... so many passing hours scarcely sensed,
today I'm breathing – ozone – and I smell
the warming bark of leafless birches
budding in the light.

I'm in a clearing when I feel
the swell inside my sunken back,
a readying of wings.

Observances: The Chapels at Paleochora

In every tiny church
a tattered mat,

an old pair of plastic
or rush-seated chairs
placed neat and straight

before the vestiges of murals.

*

We have climbed the hill
and visited fourteen,

each with its whitewashed apse

each nearer to an empty
larder than the last,

preserving on a shelf,
beside a shallow dish of oil,

thin candles for a prayer,

a water bottle much re-used

and ironed red plaid
cloth on which a faded holy image rests.

*

Outside a nearly hidden door
where fig-leaves droop

old trees are proffering
black fruit.

Fallen almonds
still in thick grey coats
dry in the dust.

★

Silver–gilt, on thorny stalks,
tall brittle weeds,

brass umbels

and a fence of blood–brown sorrel
spikes thrust from the verge

lances and arrows of desire.

★

A pilgrim's button, broken
mother of pearl, seeks to be blessed,

set down to dress a shrine.

Compelled, palms cupped,
we gather up and ferry
into cool stone rooms

simplest of gifts, the offerings.

The Deposition

A ladder has its old feet taped
to keep from scratching
parquet in the gallery.

How often it has stood there
flecked with paint, stiff as a tree,
beside the other ladder's picture

in the presence of familiar
tools from daily life:
nails, rope, bucket, knife.

From the Gods at Oz Adana, *Pas de deux*

a ritual observed

Light enough for us to see her
settling like a large gull to its ledge,
her *shalwar* faded to the once blue
colour of the bench

and light enough for him to go on
weeding rows of beans. Beneath
the vine she's shelling beans
he brought her in a basin.

Dusk gathers its brown air
above the earth they tended.
Insects hush
as bats begin to net the sky.

She goes indoors. A little light, perhaps
a single bulb, illuminates the room
where almost nothing's set
upon the table or beside their bed.

He cleans and stows his tools,
she brings outside two bowls.
A canopy of grapes is not so dense
it stops the moon

tracing their duet. Shooting stars
flare overhead and they look up.
He helps her to her feet. They step
into the garden, bowing to the night.

Pilgrimage

to the Palominos, Zippo's Circus

Unharnessed in the sun
they splay like Calder's sculptures
being placed by crane, and where they hover

muzzles scan the earth,
mole-skinned, mumbling at the turf.
One paws, another makes a stream of piss.

Heads up, one bites a rival, the pretty blond
kapok of shaken manes can't veil
big teeth which grip the gully of a corded throat.

Composed again, the tables of their spines
and buff boiled-egg behinds are suntraps,
sands smoothing dunes.

They'd overwhelm their devotees,
small girls on pilgrimage, but for CCTV and wire,
electrified, to keep the awestruck out.

The Apple Farmers' Calendar

And after all these years she wears
a skin of dirt. He didn't take her
down at the millennium,
too fond of letting his eye
run to her pale belly,

a quince compared to stripy
watermelons that block the light
beside the dented pewter bowl
weighed low by a pumpkin
heaved on the scales.

The woman at his stall
haggles for a better price
while, inches from the plank
where he wraps figs
in fig-leaves, Eve regards him

with her usual calm.
The apple in her hand
is coated in a powdering of dust,
swirled by the growers' trucks
that labour up the mountain.

Delicate, she offers it
time after time. If now and then
she slips, her painted toes
just touch the bluish paper
he keeps to parcel eggs.

Girl Running Still

Nereid Monument, British Museum

I   *If I Could Take One Home*

If I could take one home
it would be the Nereid
with seabird,

separated from the taller group
jumping at an unseen net,
playing a playground game.

In a dream they all had heads,
bright faces and blue ribbon
plaited through their hair.

Time and the dream stop,
freeze the others to their blocks.
She's still fluid as a fish,

my size, yet such a weight
I have a cradle and a winch
to lift her off the plinth.

I am not the only one
who'd want to see her as she was
at Xanthos, to take the path

from Letoon, where frogs now
fill the sacred ponds of Leto
and hills of sand the fabled harbour.

Before I reached the city gate
I'd see her stepping forward
with the other dancers celebrating

victory, lovely and unruly,
arms flung wide
between the columns

on the temple-fronted tomb,
the sea in sight and in their gift
fair winds for the voyage home.

My uncle used to say
they seemed to flurry in from bathing,
shaking off seawater.

Ankle to chin, wet
skin and almost see-through
silks like showgirls' flashed.

One he picked out as different,
more of a child still
acquiring grown-up grace.

She didn't strike a pose or try
to tame her spraying skirts.
She had to run to keep

her balance while the gull
she stood on rode the breeze.
That's how he always spoke of her – as real.

Today before I neared the usual room, a child ran up,
                stopped short, teetered
      about a metre off,
on tiptoe – in periwinkle shoes – put out his arms
as if to reach a rail
          or steady oars
                  to keep himself afloat.

Just as a water-boatman
        on the pond makes skeeterings,
so he made rings in air,
            force-fields that spun about
                his outstretched hands and newfound feet.
Those little shoes were beautiful. The stone
      he skated on was light.

        Watch me, he gestured, *I am so alive!*

          Now I'm the one who doesn't budge.
For years I've gone along to see a broken thing of stone
         and sat too often over-hot
      like any visitor in hospital, distracted
by illuminated signs, the clock, attendants.

          Which of us will change,
be first to move? She's no more
          disfigured, deaf,
            fixed in one place than I am.

From now on, let her run to me
           hooped in her cloak,
        arriving like the child.
        We'll greet each other with the same delight.

III *In the Dark and Only Now*

Come! I call, *The guardians are gone.*

  Everyone but me was counted out
at six. Only a nightwatchman
pads past, soles squeaking
on worn stone.

  And there's no need to fear
the envious eye of exit signs,
the sensor in the hygroscope.

Her room's as cold as open sky.
No moon, no-one remains
to ask what happened
  to her face, hands, hair?

In the dark and only now
I see *you* clearly!
For this is light that substitutes,

restores *your* severed arms,
the head the carver cherished
  as a daughter's
while chiselling your smile,

the tipping upwards of your chin,
      your damp curls
tightened by a salt breeze.

Fine moments, these,
you spend entire again,
returning from the sea
  across a stretch of coastline

buoyed on a gull,
your sea-wet tunic weightless
in the vacuum,

space petrified
to form a monumental volume.
Here you heal – renewed
in solid air.

IV   Stone Waves

Those men who took you from your bed
were baleful as bullocks at a gate
when they saw the Greek alight.

The quarrymen were all for downing tools
        to swig their gritty water,
                wipe the dust from dirty eyes
                        and wait
as, scrambling gecko-legged up the quarry face,
the foreign carver reached the ledge.

The foreman cursed him for insisting,
        waving unscarred hands,
                he must be first to judge
                        the fresh-split layer,
finger its white cheese,
        inspect for streaks
as if the rocks were morning-after wedding sheets.

Those men who took you from your bed
complained the blocks were wrong
for figures, too wide, too shallow,
too flat-fronted.
After they'd roughed you out,
        the last they saw of you,
                you were among a dozen lumps
trussed on a cart, wadded in straw.

They hardly gave a thought to what you'd be
in time, how far survive his treatment,
yielding to the drill, your rawness
ready for the rasp,
                nor could they know how long,
                        how many generations
– even in your ruin – you would thrill day after day:
half-dressed, damp-haired and airborne,
                                skimming stone waves.

V   *Greeting*

You still halt the young
hoping to catch the warmth
they say exists in every tongue,
assuring the beloved,
'you are beautiful'.

Your head may be on show
elsewhere, collected
from the field of war
or it may lie, face shot away,
under a Turkish road.

Your eyes will not be closed.
The lids like bezels hold
two stones that stared down
torches, smoke, white sky,
the wheeling storks of Lycia.

Standing at the station of old age,
the last light colouring
your dress, you wait,
extend a hand towards
the new arrivals.

Under the Hill

We are not single,
we are one volume: mother, child,
bound in the blind press of the beehive tomb.

We are not single.
Twenty toes seek earth, sift powder dust,
fingers stitch, spine huddles wall, fused
in the gloom before birth,

not breathing air but must.
Show us the passage, striker of light,
your tinder flares! Eyes open in the caul.

Life Class

Undressed it hardly matters
I'm unused to modelling
naked, fleshy as a prehistoric Venus
and so hot I'm grateful to be
grounded on a concrete floor
the day before my due date.

Heatwave, lava pushes
past St Martin's, penned-in
buses squeal. A diesel thermal
coils into the room and charcoal
from the life class drifts, flicks
ash across the landslips of my breasts.

At forty weeks the body's most like mud,
big with water it must shed.
I dare not shrug, adjust
a shoulder or a hip. I feel cased
in fireclay, refractory lump,
inside a clumsy jacket

fastened shut until the casting.
Let the heat work,
let the softening begin
taking with it every little detail
in the mould I've harboured:
soon this dam won't hold.

And now you

exist
outside the royal room of blood you occupied

and – without being shown –
can close a fist or yawn.

Practised, you look
already. Hopskip and bowing,
treading measure in a dance.

You only took to unfamiliar air
with your first taste of dust
yesterday as evening fell. All the falling,

all the flow around you,
hair and water, will become familiar:
mother, father: skin-to-skin.

You've swum the sea of welcome,
been lifted on the swell,
slipped waxy through the crowd of hands.

Your own breath sounded
the all-clear,
all's well,

when you sang out a first
exclamatory note

about the cord that tied you
being cut,
the tying-off, your separate knot.

Isolated Vocal Track

After the birthing hut with its bedding,
herder's carpet, close-cropped grass,
      and though we've an eye out
for markers, we're missing signs of life
except a shriek — a skidding jay —
      aptly named in Gaelic
screamer in the woods.

Sprite of the hotter climate,
all striped flash and beak, it skews,
      whisks into the prickly oak.
Must have a mate, we hear them yacking
sarcastic, solipsistic — an expletive —
      one cracks a joke, the other quips,
timing their retorts.

We skirt their wood. A silence
spreads. The mountain's ripped:
      we're staring at its wound,
an old landslide. Rocks occupy
what was a village
      emptied of sound, rocks
mute as bones.

A fractured floor, the broken
open, fallen forward
      attic bricabrac of mountain,
dust of acres slumped against survivors
of torn trees, smashed terraces, the cut
      zig of an old stone track,
zag buried under tons.

Blue dash. Black/white and pink
signals sent in rapid jerks,
        both jays' dispatches are abrupt: look up,
up, up, not at the burial ground:
forget your alpine plants, your poor head
        for heights: this is a vertical experience,
ascend the chimney of cracked light.

VIGILS

3

Landscape in Light Cast by the Moon

Tonight, as I am reading to you
one last time
Life stand still here, Mrs Ramsay said,

the Moon, white-overalled, white-masked,
is plaster casting.

Seals brooks, coats the marsh,
pours pale slip over the bay.

The cast begins to set, slowing
the sea.
          Translucence
dulls into opacity,

a plain of tented dunes
and breakers
           trapped in grey
like the fallen dog or fountains

stopped at Pompeii.

Minding the Antiquarian Bookseller's House

High on the scent of bindings, I open first editions,
leaves, more leaves. The front room is a dell of books
pushed to the ceiling, mist clinging to their spines,
the letters cut with dust.

Oh, every move is idle
                          waiting for Michael
in a house without a phone.

Down the passage there's a hotel wardrobe of a fridge,
forlorn. Two beers drunk, we dine on peanut-buttered toast.
You mouth a love song. Kiss. Natural
conclusion to a day spent on the window seat,

you on guitar, your eye on me
                        but I am waiting up for Michael.

Revealed by parting clouds, the moon snows down
on my bare legs. I say *I think I'll go to bed*. I don't intend to
sleep with you. I make a nest of cushions
on the playroom floor and though you inch inside

to make yourself at home, it's him
                         I'm waiting for
all night and wide awake. Often in an unfamiliar house I do.

From the Sleeping Car

4 a.m., Poland,
          I'm on the grey train going west
again. Smoke ghosts from stations,
               sawmills fallen silent, like the hush
                         descending on a village dance,
estranging couples
          when old fiddle-players stop.

          ....

          Dawn, train slows.

Herons tilt in blue-grey river light,
stab a crumpled eel.

          ....

Steam from a bonfire. Slight rain advances
                    over glass, greasing the silence.

A glass of tea?
You shake your head, say nothing – but your eyes
reprove me:
          don't light up:
                    yet here's a fine flame at the tip
                         and I've lit another cigarette.
Ash
fogging hand-stitched shoes – ash
               lies between us
                         who were fire and air, once
                    so fierce to couple.

We'd never sink at evening
      into cosy talk or reading... no,

as starlight dimmed we'd still be burning
          low, to embers,
             after the show. Remember *La Coupole*?

I adored those pearl-grey gloves
             I watched you peel, drawn towards
              you in the glass.

                        Why have we stopped?

A barn ablaze, fire leaping, red
             tongues above the scar of heat.

    How far we have to ride before we see
          cypresses dance, blue as gas
             at steps to our remote hotel.

        ....

    Let no-one near.
I'll need nights,
    a decent fire and silence
          if I'm to hear the song that's in the smoke,

      notes
      to finish *Nightingale*, notes to convince
             a restless Emperor
      the bird will never sleep.

God of Flame

We honoured him
at places in our home.

We kindled fires,
whole families of flame, and watched him
leap, yellow dancers
in the grate, blue on the hob.

We may have sensed
some danger at a bonfire – heat's ambush –
or perhaps we heard him brawling
in his orange tents but we were not
expecting this, the lash

when he alit
and battened on a stranger in the street,
burst through the windscreen of her fuel-doused car,
driving an inhuman cry
so raw we could not make out what
the nature of her prayer was.

Colour Beginnings

Turner's Sketchbook CCLXXXIII:
the Burning of the Houses of Parliament
16 & 17 October 1834

Up all night, until the wind changed,
with but four colours to hand.
At seven on the Strand smelled smoke, fancied
I heard Trojans in the firecarts' bells.

Filled my flask at the Adelphi steps
and hailed Old Booth. He rowed the tender
crabwise across the Lambeth mud,
secured it and scuttled off. Tide out,

mud and hawsers bronzed in the furnace light.
Before me blazed the last trump or sunset
on the Nile, the burning Houses a foreign fleet.
I've seen every yellow Earth can conjure,

yet I had only one, and though I've made it match
a sunrise, brimstone, saffron, sulphur,
even jaundice, I thought it insufficient here –
those palaces were cracked crucibles, leaking red gold.

Just as well I had the fierce vermilion
since Everyman above me on the bridge
was tanned a redskin, African, Indian,
joining the procession from our dominions.

From under stovepipe hats and shawls swelled
a great stare of faces, leonine, red earthenware,
roaring, *There, Sirs, go your Reforms!*
White bonnets were like helmets, some bloodied.

All this I got down, scribbled, sponged, stained.
Yet I wished there was a better black than lamp
black to serve for that charred mass, damned dark
the orange tongues had lapped, ash, soot, slag.

Lit up throughout the night the sky demanded blue,
more blue, a pan of cobalt – fire-bright,
smutted, greasy. I smeared it with my thumbs
and Ma Booth's cloth that wraps the pie

she always stows inside the bailer, reckoned
I'd more need. Leafing through my notes today
I find a cinder, blown downwind, has lodged its mark
before the paint had time to dry.

At the Root of the Wind is Strife

according to Empedocles

after dark

sevenish, December, when a reveller on the South Bank lifts a bag,
                    opens it, out sneaks – freed

from the mythic bag of winds – a hungry gust with a taste for plastic
                    wrap and smeared empties

after weeks of diet: crazy for a lick at cans lodged in the crook
                    of evergreens. Enter, inebriated

wind round midnight, now to leap and beat as waves do, reaching
                    house fronts, occasionally gale

force, upstart alarms and make the sirens weep.

daylight

                    Twelve hours on, the morning
mind's so tuned to monochrome it dwells on carcrash,

                    intimations of fatality.
A garden's unnerved, pinched beneath the flight path;

                    if roses could despair,
they'd sink this low, ashen, winter-worsened.

                    Two police whichwaydegoes
increase in whush, very rapid and another hornlike,

                    dooda dooda, as it spins,
whirling Catherine wheel of earsplit, banshee band.

daylong

Air over London is a mountain
tunnelled through with din, draughts down every stack and chimney,

mineshafts,
squeal, clank, crashed gears, thumped drums. Workers wield a thousand

picks and hammers,
tocktock, gamelan tingtang, staccato clock tick, clock on, clock off,

ambulances' rising whistles
ripple east flingflingaling to new emergency quick birth attack or fire

accelerating. Bully wind
                and bully's patter runs to bellow, bluster.

dark again

Hanged woman on the street, neck noosed by her long hair,
                  man with pent-up pitbull

shrinks from the rain's harangue, the quaking glass in walls.
                  Bus tides suck and swirl

delivering crocodiles in gutters. Thunder in gouts, all hail
                  on windscreens, buckshot

diamonds pock and tag, the final push at nineteenhundred.
                  Landing craft and minicabs

attend the mess, the muddled men, the downed, drowned-out,
                  sound-sickened in the day-long skirmish.

Single Figures

Too many statues are solitary men.
                    Some of them, the grand
old dukes and generals who rode an elegant mount,
were skied on plinths
                    high over cab-horses,
above the heads of crowds,
        though nowadays the people on the top
deck of a bus glance at them
sideways.
            Sometimes the island
loneliness is right, the wait and cold,
wet weight of the sergeant standing
at Hyde Park, his oilskin
pockets out of shape
                    with keepsakes, pipe,
his letters bundled in a map.

The Realism of Late Roman Portraits

They're all facing one way
with the air of an assembly
gathered for an expert speaker
at the late-night-opening Glyptothek.

When no-one of importance steps up
to a dais, mouths purse, their marble jaws clamp.

Heads, or rather busts – on stands
chest-high – the powerful were shorter then –
turn back to contemplating those they used to greet:
exiles, ruling families disgraced,
suicides: they must have known
at heart it was the end for Rome.

Although their eyes are drilled and white
they darken: winter on a Northern lake in sleet.

Solo

Island Observance

While wind cuts trenches in the sea, no body
goes to hallowed ground. The coffin's sheltered
on a ledge, north-facing, no man's land, turned
towards the churchyard – but a week may pass
in waiting till the curragh's launched.

Indoors, by the smoke of mutton fat
swilling around the wick in scallop shells,
a cousin reaches for a larger teapot,
more of the kept-for-best chipped cups:
there's talk of how the wedding was,

a coat from Dingle, letters from America,
the teacher, words to fiddle tunes. Another
cousin pats a handed-down oiled cap
and they're all waiting for a drop
in wind, listening to the waves.

Outside, only the departed is denied
familiar company, a soul arrested on a rock
enduring hours Blasket islanders must lie
apart, above the sea, cold as the stone field
they honour as *the place of loneliness*.

Emergency Landing

When tiny cowries slink into my shoes
and grains of coral grit between my toes,

wake me. Let me see
in daylight pink's the colour of the sand

I'm stepping in. And may the water be
turquoise and the palm trees

standing straight, not crashing
sideways as we hit an island.

★

Go back to the moment in the circling plane
  we spot the ocean playing

with a rope of emeralds at its throat.
My mother's fierce eyes fix on one,

enlarging, as on prey.
A landing strip, wet at both ends

with nets, long skiffs, men
leaving for the night, their faces tipped

towards us in the air
– in song or prayer – calling to Allah?

★

Night briskly shuts
the lid of violet sky. We clutch

our bears, heads pushed down
for the plunge, my sister's being sick,

and someone shrieks
stop! A stink of burning. *Stop!*

★

Uncurl, so long
curled up, it hurts.

★

After the ocean's stare
we cannot meet men's eyes,

ours hug the beach.
Blanched in torchlight, we steer shy

of hands reaching to help us to the hut
where we are put to bed

only to dive again in sleep.

4

ENTER THE SEA

We all were sea-swallowed, though some cast again
The Tempest

Enter the Sea

                    not, you understand,
as water – but as close as it can come without a liquid
inrush at your ear – intimacy tantamount
to sleeping with you.
                    Breathing's urgent, always
that impatience, hurried intakes, under-muttered
tug. Settled only for the hour before dawn, before
the volume's up again and your pulse triples,
tricked:
            you hear it on the hammered stairs
climbing to demand attention in your bed.
The sea insists upon rehearsing its peculiar score,
replaying in high wind the hardest passages
so audio intense
                    they speed your heart, contract/expand
the space in sea-struck rooms about your head.

As It Was

I could go back along the clouded path
in my sleep or blindfolded. I'd know the way

we always walked in summer,
follow the familiar rite of shoe removal

when I reached the brook
before the sands. But there's no sea

in sight, the sky's closed down.
A hood is pulled over the coast,

rocks are caped and furred
in white, dense and wet with light.

Ahead the boys and Chrissie slide
into the nebula. Nothing's as it was.

At the Dew Pond, West Dale

The boys have caught the sun
and cross the field with their loot,
striding barefoot on cropped grass,
surf-boards like shields held triumphal,
four crowns laurelled by the cliff-edge light.
The sea's a wily dog who tugs them back:
swinging to face its pull they stall, lose all
sense of being watched.
                       A tiny snake
weaves through the cool purée of pond,
black-buttoned in its shift of greenness.
First time we've ever seen one
here, long evenings waiting for our young –
who happen on us suddenly as men.

The Shift

Even between sisters
delicacy lasts.

So it may go unmentioned, years,
the moment when things changed.

The night,
the party mood, the eyes.

Do you still have that dress, my sister asks,

(the dress which flowed when dancing
cider wild on New Year's Eve)

the one you wore into the sea?

(A summer dress and insubstantial,
more of a veil or net, dark indigo with tendrils
drawn in seaweed green.

Wet, it caught
the wink of paddle steamers
hung with Christmas lights, late out to Ryde.)

She must have guessed.

I tell her how the muslin
clung and hobbled me and washed against our legs

when he and I had gone
waist-deep across the prickly shelf
of giants' toenail shells.

She nods. You dragged it like a fishtail off the beach.

And as for him, his pale feet were pointed,
see-through with cold, like fins.
She adds, his beautiful transparent flesh.

Lucky, you only lost
the feeling in your hands,

you could have caught your death.

Of Vertigo

Too much time already lost, not enough – the officer was firm –
for lifeboats, even if it was *Man Overboard*, or child.
My mother yelled at the assembling crowd
For God's sake, DO something. Look!
But out of eyes of stone so heavy my head sank,
I looked and only saw a whitish scribble
wash along the ship's steel wall below.
And thought maybe I saw a wild gang
of small hands claw, scrabble for the rail.
I couldn't lift my feet, hooked to the deck
by hackles risen on the spines of planks.
Somehow stood erect enough to *look*,
yet not connect the wake of toppling
glass, the starboard shadow or
the churning in the ocean's
bowl of light.

It was the first I knew
of vertigo, first sense of void,
the mind blue-blank, blood draining
from the heart, a body not belonging.
Strings – my puppet joints unstrung
– looped down, unweighted, thin,
entering the ocean's pattern after
him, small secret child, brother
with a liking for the Oriental
carpet of the sea, fractals
flowering perpetually.

Sallyport

Ramparts hid the Solent, had the tide-race
channelled tight. In gales chimneys shrank
behind stone towers, within the enceinte
of redbrick Naval walls that closed off cobbled
streets. Telescopes alone craned for a view
from upper bays on Grand Parade and Battery
Row.

        Sent to get a change of air, I slipped
head down through the sea-door and met a squall
that stung so hard I didn't see the breaker
swell and swing.

              I felt its wrestling heave,
the shingle flung like sleet, a thud against
the beach. This wave I square up to at night,
it throws itself —

              I brace to take the weight.

After the Ban

A spring tide
          pigged on wrack
                              has strewed   *its picnic*
hard-sucked orange   *bleach*   *flasks*
                              peppermint creamcleaners

Perhaps
if they were
cleaned
they
would appeal
to a collector,
these vessels,
slim
as Cycladic
dolls,
tar-spangled,
vaguely familiar,
some a little more
pneumatic,
all precious
because we
have no
plastic.

abraded lemon grime-removers   *red bitten*
                                                      teats of sports drinks
          suntan lotions   *weather-beaten*
                                  toilet ducks   *along the beach*

We need
the old
capacious
baskets
folk called creels,
sturdy and curved
as clamshells
to gather in
the spill.
But we
have only
swimming bags
we've woven
from flag
iris leaves.
And then
we see
the whale.

The Sea is Midwife to the Shore

A bay is giving birth within black walls of rain,
            waves grasping sky, threatening
    the cliff. There's barely any beach

        and there'll be no more
            you and I
                strip-washed, when the swell

    erases us and swallows
            from the sand our footprints
                            with the view wiped

                grey, a shaken Etch-a-Sketch,   demagnetised
except for tiny dits
                    – and dashes – on a chart of cove.

    It's then the sea smoothes,
                fondles chubby stones, croons over each
                            peculiar stone and treats it
    as its own
        newborn, immense and gleaming,
                    nursed on the stretched belly of the beach.

House at Sea

on the Camber, Old Portsmouth

How high the tide's been hoisted –
inside the chandlers' shop on Broad Street,
across the whaler–builders' yard –
swirling rotted rope and scales about
the harbour, milky as an oyster.
Stew-brown tarpaulin drips,
the caul of what lies long in dry dock.

Sea tugs at the mooring of our house,
which turns away its blinkered bay front
from the Solent. We must sit out the winter
behind salt-swollen doors, curtains smouldering
with damp, stiff in a cummerbund of fog
while – in the passage, underneath the boards –
we hear waves stomp and smack the cellar wall.

My father lifts the hatch. I watch the dark
green creature claw the bottom step
and mount. Eyes and 'o's of diesel,
winking, double on the swell. Uneasy
in the light the water rears, recoils
and lunges, spitting at the lantern
swinging from my father's hand.

Nelson's Last Walk

14 September 1805

At noon he nips away on foot (to dodge
admirers) over Governor's Green and up
the ramparts, through the tunnel. At the bridge
he'll hail the barge, be rowed out to his ship.
Huzzas rise from the crowds on King's Bastion,
the mound they climbed to catch sight of the fleet
across the fort's Long Curtain batteries
(which locals call Hot Walls) beyond the moat.

Even the Hero of the Nile cannot
leave shore from these high loaves of Portland stone,
that form a white hill, polished now by grit
spat out by Solent storms, serried in the sun –
but scurries down the beach to quit his England
before the flood tide ebbs and stains the shingle.

Sea View and Separation, Sole Bay

I

      At windows where there's nothing to the east but sea,
    we take our seats and wait. You will not talk. You haven't slept
though when you came indoors, you cried for sleep

     – and maybe sleep is out there in the lull that's fallen on the bay –

       but every wave subsiding sighs a note of doubt,
          an anxious yield, and drops it
             on the beach as it repeats its pebble-count.

II

We both keep very still, our heads erect,
avert our gaze. Between the transom and the sill
there is the glass:

                  on it may stay his eye;
                  or if he pleaseth, through it pass,
                  and then the heaven espy

the line of the horizon's
    pencilled flat, exact,
        air above it,

    _____

       sea below, ruled and tense. It defines
          the long oblong, open waters' band of brown

scored like a school-room floor,
    coarse-grained:

       bottom left, a mat of surf rucks,
     wrinkles where it reaches shore.

III

In the glass-sided tank of night
we are adrift like fish without the drift to sleep.

       Lift my chin at dawn to a blank
       postcard sky (AFFIX STAMP, ADDRESS). You have gone.

Look down, see the beaten
garden, how a few cold flowers stand the salt.

       A concrete post holds out
       its white P, *piano*, abbreviated quiet.

The sea's *piano*,
frieze without sound:

       slow-motion rituals of early morning on the beach
       begin with little noise, puddling

flecks of mousse in water, white swill
flick flick, birds, sharp-edged blades.

IV

Tuning, the sound's turned up.
Juvenile gulls start shrieking and the sea-beat
compounds the irritation of an angry man –
                        bang!
note the force with which he shuts his car third time.

Waves test and throw grey weights
against the shingle. I watch a solitary swimmer.

He swam all summer every day, all weathers. Strip, strike out
but not come back, who could do that?

Some things don't change in a seaside town:
a black dog's worrying a piece of net. *Fetch, Ruby,*
Ruby, here!
               She's bounding seaward
                  past where fish-shacks
peter out and where the beach displays its old exhibits:

pale-as-the-dead seaweed, glaucous cabbage, picked
bones, mermaid's purse, a careful rounding-up of pebbles.

Always the percussive trudge, walkers striking
over brassy stones, down to the wash and grit.

V

Sun riffles the grey ream of waves.
        Light comes and goes, nothing is fixed,
blue eye appears through cloud, is closed.

Rain pats the animal that is the sea,
        leads the tide home along the estuary,
to rest in reeds, salt waterland.

Vacancies are hung at windows in Sole Bay.
        A flapping crow lands,
hooded pilgrim, standing man.

Stay

A man that looks on glass,
On it may stay his eye;
Or if he pleaseth, through it pass
— George Herbert

Take me, a woman at a window, how
do I look? Climbing on the sill, press face
and body to the pane. The sea shoots up
like mercury to a line below my eye.

Eight miles at least to the horizon now
I gauge from my new height, but I don't sweep
the view as if it were a field, I'm caught:
the world out there presents a sheer wall.

Cold arrests me, bars my mouth. Draughts
tighten round my ribs and bind me to
the brittle sheet vibrating in the wind.

Glass fuses with my skin. Its thinness
is no barrier, unmanned
frontier through which I let the sea.

The Crossing

A wall of water in the dark pours
loosely on a runway or a road – so much
released, it isn't obvious that here's a man
until he nears.
                  Three floodlights stop him
at the verge where he must cross,
his temples bathed in rain, his garments
steeping, shining, heavy laden.

He walks towards me, watching,
while I shift, standing my dry ground,
and though his hands declare him
luggageless, he's charged
– as I am charged with witnessing
how he will bear the fall of water,
pass through the wall of mourning.

Again (reprise)

Rain set in at six, waves flecked
like wet tweed, heavy trousers, hoisted
with a webbing belt, sky a pale shirt which shed
its light. Bit by bit it fluttered into ash,
until almost everything was lost
from sight, when – and I did not appreciate
how far, the distance you had come –
you reappeared. Believing no-one
could be out that night in their right mind
I did not want to open then. And yet
I let you in. I would again.

Notes

'Against This Light'
After Léon Cogniet, *First Letter from Home, the Artist Reading in his Room at the Villa Medici*, 1817. His sister too would become a painter and teacher of life drawing to women barred from attending classes for male art students.

'Patient at Paimio'
In the early twentieth century an unusually high incidence of recovery from TB was recorded at Paimio, a sanatorium designed by Alvar Aalto in a remote forest in Finland.

'Girl Running Still'
The Nereid Monument (so called after the Nereids, mythical daughters of wind and sea gods) was removed to the British Museum from Xanthos in southwest Turkey, once a wealthy city of Lycia. The fragmented dancing figures had fallen from a temple façade, thought to have been a tomb commissioned by the city's Persian satrap, or governor, who died c. 380 BC. It stood overlooking the approach from the great harbour of Patara and the much visited temple complex at Letoon.

'Single Figures'
Ordinary soldiers and the dead of WWI are depicted at the Royal Artillery Memorial by Charles Sargeant Jagger at Hyde Park Corner. Jagger himself fought at Gallipoli and in northern France.

'The Crossing'
After Bill Viola, *The Crossing (Water)*, 1996, video installation exhibited at the National Gallery, London, 2003.

Acknowledgements

Thanks are due to the editors of the following in which poems appeared: *Ambit, Hic et Nunc (Poetry on the Lake), Long Poem Magazine, New Walk, New Welsh Review, Poetry Review, Poetry Salzburg Review, The Reader, The Red Wheelbarrow, The Rialto, Seam, South Bank Poetry, The Stinging Fly, The Times Literary Supplement* and *Warwick Review*.

'The Apple Farmers' Calendar' was selected for *Best British Poetry 2011* (Salt, ed. Roddy Lumsden). 'Colour Beginnings' and 'Emergency Landing' were first published in *Bedford Square 2* (John Murray, 2007, ed. Andrew Motion).

'After the Ban' won the inaugural Edwin Morgan International Poetry Prize in 2008, a generous award which enabled me to complete my PhD. I am also grateful to Simon Trewin and the late Pat Kavanagh for the PFD Student Award to study at Royal Holloway, University of London in 2006/7.

Special thanks are due to Jo Shapcott, Andrew Motion, Stephen Knight and Greta Stoddart; to readers of poems at an early stage: Fiona Moore, Helen Adie, Rupert Christiansen and Greg Penoyre; to Christopher Le Brun for suggesting a painting for the cover; and to my editor at Oxford Poets, Iain Galbraith.